Get Ready.
Get Set.
Flow...

Get Ready.
Get Set.
Flow...

Work/Life Integration for
Soul-Powered People

Christine Clifton

Mindful Business Press

www.MindfulBusinessPress.com

Christine Clifton
Saxapahaw, North Carolina
Christine@ChristineClifton.com, www.ChristineClifton.com
(201) 738-7463

Requests for permission or further information should be addressed to:

Mindful Business Press
Christine@ChristineClifton.com

Cover Artwork
Valerie Herald

To Cheryl Mucha and Bruce Arbit:
Thank you for trusting me as this body of work unfolded.
Watching you both grow is one of my greatest joys.
Love you!

Table of Contents

Acknowledgements

To Stephanie: Four years ago you planted the seed that these concepts needed brought into the world in a much bigger way. You've been an integral part of this book's development. Who woulda thunk, 30 years ago, that we'd be here today? Love you!

To my "The Connection Experiment" Supporters: You rocked my world, thank you SO much!

To Kurt and Janet: Pre-reading this book and giving me feedback was priceless, thanks!

To my family, friends, and clients: Your support means the world to me. Thank you for enabling me to bring my true value, my sacred work, and my full self into the world.

To those who influenced me, my beliefs, and my writings: Parker J. Palmer, Gary Douglas, Michael Singer, Simon Sinek, Rhonda Byrne, Marianne Williamson, John Randolph Price, Matt Licata, Jeff Foster, Jeff Brown, Neville Goddard, Abraham Hicks, Byron Katie, and so many more. Bringing your great work into the world, even amongst the naysayers, has given me the courage to bring forth mine.

Introduction

I believe that work/life balance is a myth. You can keep adding on activities on both sides of that scale and still be in balance, although quite burdened. And who decided, anyway, that there are only two categories? In the life category are things like family activities, volunteerism, spiritual/religious groups, neighborhood and community participation, hobbies, and charity support. For most people, the life category is much more active and full than the work category.

A greater level of spiritual "surrender" has brought me and my clients much closer to our connection to "the Source of our understanding" (whether we call it God, The Universe, Spirit...) and allowing our true natures to more fully show up in our work lives. Here forward, I use the terms Source and Spirit interchangeably.

The concepts in this book are a presentation of my perspective for integrated living instead of striving for unattainable work/life balance. As Parker J. Palmer positions, living "divided no more" in his book *A Hidden Wholeness*.

One of the most powerful practices with my clients is helping them broaden the scope of their lives so that their work, whether they work for a company or own one, is just one part of it. They are making themselves the center point of their lives instead of their work. They are feeding their souls so they can serve.

Soul-powered entrepreneurs and professionals are heeding the call of our Purpose or Why – I call it our sacred calling. This willingness to be a conduit for others' benefit is what I mean by soul-powered service. Understanding the interplay of your BEing-ness with your DOingness is critical in order to fully tap into the possibilities and reSources available to you to fulfill that calling.

Instead of looking at things in a work/life balance perspective, you're integrating your full self in all aspects of your life. This brings a greater alignment with your true nature and enables you to be more agile when faced with a pivot point – and that facilitates flow.

No matter your spiritual beliefs, I invite you to open your mind to the concepts here and translate them so they feel aligned for you. In short, *Get Ready. Get Set. Flow...* flips the traditional paradigm of fitting into our environment and shows how aligning your outer DOing to your inner BEing facilitates opportunities, creativity, and fulfillment in your life and work.

CHAPTER ONE

Are You a Soul-Powered Person?

If you hear the call to service, you're likely soul-powered. We feel compelled to serve. We're heart-centered, highly relational, and love to help others. We anticipate others' needs and enjoy the acknowledgement we receive. We care deeply about what others think of us. We're driven by mission not by money. We believe in a higher power.

With that light, also comes some shade: we often give to others at the detriment of ourselves. We want to serve so much, that we might undercut our value just so we can. We put a lot of burden on our business or career to provide for us. We have a tumultuous relationship with money. We let others' reactions to us guide our decisions.

If any of those characteristics ring true for you, then you're likely a soul-powered person.

Being soul-powered acknowledges that we are souls in a physical experience right now. Our soul is the connection to the Source. Source is driving us through life using our soul like a rear-wheel drive sports car. We're being strongly moved along by a power greater than us because our soul is ever-evolving. It's almost as if we can't help but do what we do. It's inevitable because our soul is predestined to evolve. That is, unless we get in its way.

We get in its way when we try to make something happen that's not aligned. Force feels like being in a front-wheel drive compact car. We keep trying to do something to make it go faster. We're using a lot of effort to get things done. We feel frustrated when something slows us down or seemingly gets in the way. We're running around trying anything because we figure something's got to stick. Sound familiar?

The soul-powered-ness of our BEing is our secret superpower. With our belief in the Source of our understanding, we know that we have this energy at play on our behalf. Yet, we most commonly use it only in our service to others. Most people don't know how – or don't feel comfortable – using its full power on their own behalf.

Without it, you aren't showing up fully in the world – intentional or not. Without it, you aren't getting everything you want out of life and work. Without it, you aren't being fully authentic. Without it, you're missing out on the infinite possibilities of The Universe.

The word vocation is rooted in the Latin word for "voice." It's not a goal. It's not work. It's a calling that you hear. Parker J. Palmer says in his book *Let Your Life Speak* that "before I can tell my life what I want to do with it, I must listen to my life telling me who I am."

As a dance teacher, I love this line from John Michael Montgomery: "Life's a dance, you learn as you go. Sometimes you lead and sometimes you follow." You can see my "both/and" philosophy here, too. Not only do we lead our life, but it also sometimes leads us. Not only do we lead our work/business, but it also sometimes leads us.

One of my coaches was the first person to show me what he saw as a theme in my motivation and work. It's common not to see those themes ourselves, because we are too close to them and because we don't typically compare ourselves to others. We are simply moving through the world, doing our great work. We must listen to our lives telling us who we are. We must be ready to follow it when it guides us.

The magic question I have for you is this: "How agile are you to pivot when life or work wants to lead you?"

If you don't have this agility, it could be why you're not meeting your life/work goals. Agility is at the core of Flow. If you were to choose just one focus, I would tell you to work on your agility skills. Agility cannot happen without proper alignment. Neither can happen without knowing how. Neither can happen without practice.

CHAPTER TWO

My Evolution as a Soul-Powered Person

In 2008, I left my corporate career to start my first business. Since then, I've organically evolved my body of work and the services I offer. I went from having a coaching practice for women with chronic illness, to owning a brick and mortar wellness studio, to providing business development services for solopreneurs, to consulting and teaching business development skills and processes for service entrepreneurs and firms, to supporting corporate professionals in their career and leadership growth, to becoming a fractional business partner to owners of small professional services firms.

At first, I judged myself for not sticking to any one thing; for not being focused; and for being all over the place. When I decided to close my wellness studio after only 13 months, people said to me, "Christine, a business takes at least three years to ramp up, you should stay open." One colleague even said to me once, "Christine, you don't seem to stick to one thing. You've got to give it time to take hold."

I can look back now and see that my intuition was guiding me. I wrestled with it, for sure, because those well-meaning voices shared traditional business truths. There was just something nudging at me that told me those truths weren't for me. I now know what was happening was that I was allowing myself to fully embody my spiritual self into my work self. I realized that all of my changes were less about lack of focus and more about embracing how I was unfolding into the world. Everything we do is based on "who we be."

As I let go of the self-judgement, I began to ease more smoothly into my own life and work. After introducing it to my clients, I saw incredible results in their work as well as in their lives. I purposefully use both of those terms because, as soul-powered people, who we are anywhere is who we are everywhere.

In mid-2014, I rebranded my company, Client Centric Growth, to Mindful Business Matters. My business coach at the time advised me against it, saying that no one would understand what it means. I knew for sure it was the right name to use and I took a small first step to better align my business with me.

I chose "Mindful" because I felt it was an accessible word that had become more mainstream in business. In addition, the name reflected the fact that I was now working with corporate professionals and companies, not just service entrepreneurs. It was a step closer to flow.

In early 2016, I was inspired by a book called *The Surrender Experiment* by Michael Singer and a body of work called Access Consciousness™. I began to incorporate some of those practices into my own life and was experiencing major personal and business growth.

In my work at that time, I was primarily working with solo service entrepreneurs as a business development consultant who specialized in in-person business activities. As situations arose with my clients, I began to introduce the new concepts to them as well.

In short, I began to incorporate belief, mindset, and personal growth coaching into the mix. Not only was I was expanding and evolving yet again, but my clients were also experiencing growth in their lives, businesses, and careers. The group of concepts you'll be learning about in this book are those I've developed and made my own.

Because of the steady evolution of my body of work with my clients, I'm often challenged to adequately describe the kind of work that I do. While everyone's belief systems are slightly different, most of my kindred spirit network at least believes in The Law of Attraction, The Secret, "Like attracts like." Or "What you think about, you bring about."

One of my clients tells people that I put the "how-to" to the "woo-woo." Meaning, all of my practical methods and approaches are supported by Law of Attraction and spiritual principles. Another phrase I use that catches people's attention is "Keep your inner fire burning so you don't burn out," because it speaks to the importance of fulfillment and meaning.

Along the path of my entrepreneurship, I discovered several of my own unique gifts of seeing themes, sensing energy behind motivations, and quickly seeing the B.S. (belief system) that holds people back.

At first, it felt odd to incorporate the therapeutic B.S.-shifting work with my clients, because I had become known as the business development "how-to" expert for service entrepreneurs. Yet, when my clients weren't implementing the how-to actions, I could "see" the reasons why: it was their B.S. If they kept doing what they'd always done, they were going to keep getting what they'd always gotten. It was my responsibility to lovingly show them what I saw and give them the choice to heal the root cause.

The soul-powered entrepreneurs and professionals that I work with have many interests. I call them creatives: not all of them are artists, musicians, or dancers – though some are. They are all, however, creative thinkers. I also call them spiral thinkers. Their minds work in a beautifully random manner, like a butterfly's flight path. Like me, most were cultured to believe that isn't the "right" way to be – that they need to pick one thing. Over time, a little shame appears because, no matter how hard they try, they keep reverting back to the "wrong" behaviors.

Yet, I believe that there's absolutely nothing wrong with having many interests – it is actually their natural way of being. In their thoughts and behaviors, they're in the process of creating. All that's typically needed is the slightest bit of infrastructure, framework, or architecture in order to keep them directionally correct. As a Virgo, I rock at creating these structures.

I now know that the uniqueness of me is what draws people to me. The more comfortable I am to share my wholeness, the more people who hear me and experience me will realize that they no longer have to hide, either. I am the conduit, so I cannot ignore that I am an influential element of their success.

I teach adults the joy of social partner swing dancing, Carolina Shag, and West Coast Swing. The concepts and approach to teach adults how to swing dance, how to move their body when they've not danced before, is an esoteric concept. I'm really good at teaching dance. Dancing facilitates a connection with your mind, body, and spirit. A social dance is a three-minute conversation – a three-minute relationship.

In addition to my coaching, consulting, guidance, and mentoring work, I'm evoking a book out of one of my clients. I write poetry and create guided visualizations. I help a client interview and onboard new employees. I co-host a neighbor night gathering in my village. I create social media posts for a client in her voice. I'm a creative, too.

What is the common theme in all that I do? Me. I am the common theme. I am the center point. How I do anything is how I do everything. My sacred calling is to keep human connection alive through the art of conversation. I'm a teacher of transformation and a facilitator of flow. I am a creative. It's how I show up in my whole life, not just in my work. It's all about connection. It's all about humans. It's all about stimulating connection to Source, Self, and Service.

> *"The paradox of discipline is that it enables creativity."*
> —QUAKER FAITH & PRACTICE

A musician can't write a song until she knows the chords and music theory. A dancer can't choreograph a work until he learns the basic steps and positions. The "discipline" of the concepts and practices you'll learn in this book will enable you the freedom that you crave as a soul-powered person of service.

Each section invites you to learn about the concept through teaching, real examples of the application of the concept in my and my clients' lives, and thought-provoking questions and exercises so you can begin to bring the concept into inspired action for yourself.

CHAPTER THREE

The Benefits of Alignment and Agility

You've probably heard or used planning tools at some point in your life or work. Whether it's a day planner or planning software, I have a hunch that you never really enjoyed using something like that. Many soul-powered people push back when it comes to actually plotting out how you're going to move through your career or business.

The last two years I was in corporate, I was the sales coach for a 100-person commercial sales division in my company. Part of my duties was helping them write and implement business plans and sales plans. As a result, I know a little something about planning.

I wrote a great business plan for my first business and it lived in a file cabinet somewhere. I remember coming across it much later and seeing that I had implemented the majority of what I planned. Plans are definitely one way of visioning what you want to do, but there was something I was missing, I could feel it.

After four years of bumbling through entrepreneurship, I realized I needed to know more about what I was trying to do. I decided to join a year-long group coaching program for entrepreneurs that cost $10,000. At the end of that year, I felt spit out on the other side, completely burnt out and almost broke. I was doing everything right, yet few of the practices they taught me had worked for me. I was so frustrated, that in the last group meeting of that one-year program, I asked the founder of the program, "What do you suggest to overcome marketing burnout?"

The meeting was a video livestream with 100 other entrepreneurs. You know what she said to me? She said, "You must not be cut out for entrepreneurship, then, if you're burnt out." I was incredulous. I paid her $10,000; implemented everything I was taught; and that's all she had to say.

That was a real pivot point in my life and work. It sent me down a spiral of depression because I had taken the leap of faith to make that investment in myself, and now I was almost broke. It was a very dark time for me. I even questioned whether there really was a higher-power or if The Universe truly had my back.

Somewhere deep inside of me, though, I heard this little voice of Spirit in my heart and I knew there had to be another way. I just knew there was – and I was going to figure it out! I struck out from that rock-bottom place and began to use my gift of seeing themes and what makes things work.

I was able to see that the $10,000 program absolutely worked for the woman who launched it – and it worked for her because it was her unique business model. She had discovered what worked for her and she made a model out of it.

I saw that it didn't work for me because so much of it wasn't aligned with my personal value system and how I wanted to treat people. I saw that the messaging they developed for me wasn't my true and authentic voice. I saw the activities they had me doing weren't a fit for my style and personality.

Traditional career-search and business growth models rarely fully work for soul-powered people. Why? Because each and every one of us is an absolutely unique human being. Who you are, what your strengths are, what your calling is, what your preferences are, and who you're here to serve are all a unique comingling of elements that are at play in your reality alone.

In addition, you have the power of Source in your toolbelt, which brings infinite possibilities. When you take the time to align your DOing with your BEing, it gives you the agility to pivot when something aligned comes along that you didn't plan for. As a result, no set model is going to work well for you because it doesn't account for the unexpected.

That being said, I do believe in the power of "both/and." There are some proven truths out there in business, so we shouldn't throw the baby out with the bathwater. However, instead of putting them into a cookie-cutter model, they are better used as a method within a framework of aligned inspired action.

Don't get me wrong. I didn't say to not ever plan or make a vision board. I'm not saying don't ever put milestones on your goal sheet. What I *am* saying is that you have the opportunity to integrate your soul-powered BEing into your DOing in order to invite expansion into your experience.

Burnout was named an occupational phenomenon in 2018 by the World Health Organization. It's not caused by doing too much. It's caused by DOing things that are out of alignment with your BEing. The root of the word "wealth" is "well-being or welfare." On the path to earn more money and make a bigger difference, many professionals and entrepreneurs are driving themselves into the ground.

Your health is the fuel to support your great service in the world. Soul-powered people often skip over themselves in order to serve. That behavior is out of alignment because we can't successfully serve others while bypassing our own needs, wants, and dreams. Doing so causes burnout, stagnancy, and stuck-in-a-rut-ness.

As someone who has suffered with chronic illness the majority of her adult life, I know firsthand the impact of poor health. Mine is rooted in a connective tissue dysfunction, so it impacts my whole body. I've learned how to make everything I do more efficient and effective with these integrative concepts so that I don't overtax myself.

You don't have to choose between service and self. You don't have to choose between mission and money. You can choose "both/and." In fact, it's an imperative to nurture your own uniqueness because Source is working through you so that you can serve. Integrating your true nature brings more ease into all that you do. Your stress levels go down and your fulfillment grows. My clients say they feel less worry and more peace because they trust their intuition and their decision-making.

The *Get Ready. Get Set. Flow...* paradigm demonstrates the power of "both/and." It's both preparation in the practical sense and also allowance in the spiritual sense. It's the integration of those that fuels your agility.

CHAPTER FOUR

The Four Orbs of Soul-Powered Living

I often hear people say things like "I've just got to trust The Universe." Or "I know God is going to get me out of this." Or "Why am I not getting what I want? I'm doing all the right things."

Soul-powered people cannot live a divided life. All of those statements contain elements of separateness. Saying you've got to trust The Universe is ridiculous because it has no free will. It's really about trusting yourself. Saying God will get you out of something is ridiculous because it might be an experience you're supposed to be having. It's really about trusting your sacred calling. Thinking that doing all the right things will get you what you want is ridiculous because doing is just one element. It's really about why you want what you want and how you feel about the things you want.

Just like The Law of Attraction is only one of many Laws of the Universe, its metaphysics is only one of several energetic orbs at play on soul-powered people. The four orbs are Spiritual, Metaphysical,

Physical, and Emotional and they are all at play in our reality at all times.

Spiritual

Your spiritual beliefs are a part of who you are. If you're like me, they've ebbed and flowed over the years as I've evolved. I believe that I'm a particle of the divine walking this planet. Every time I interact with others is a divine experience because they are experiencing Source through me. This belief is tied to the importance of realizing your sacred calling: what your purpose (or Why) is here on this planet.

There is some crossover between Spiritual and Metaphysical in my interpretation. For example, the spiritual belief that "we are all one" is behind the concept of "like attracts like." Think of the big bang theory, that everything started from one form. Think of what Jesus says in the Bible, that what you do to your brother, you do to yourself.

Think about your spiritual beliefs: how are you using them in life and work?

Metaphysical

Traditionally, metaphysics is defined as "beyond physics." Today the word has grown into a lot of different interpretations. I'm using it in the context of The Law of Attraction, "like attracts like" and "what you think about, you bring about." Therefore, it's about how you're attuning your vibrational frequency so that you attract what you choose.

Manifesting is a concept that I see getting skewed in interpretation. The word "manifest" was originally a noun: think of a ship's manifest. Manifest means inventory, a list of belongings. Everything you need is already here; all you have to do is call it in.

Think about your metaphysical beliefs: how are you using them in life and work?

Physical

As soul-powered people, we are living in a body in a physical world. Our physical presence is what allows us to fulfill our sacred calling. In these bodies, we might experience pain or pleasure. We experience other human beings, animals, and plants in this physical existence. Quantum physics proves that everything is energy and what we see in this physical world is energy so dense that it's visible.

Observing what's happening with the circumstances, objects, and people around you gives you clues and information about how energy is showing up around you in alignment with your vibration.

Think about your physical experience: how are you using it in life and work?

Emotional

Where there is emotion, there is learning. Emotions are signals for growth. Many of us weren't raised with healthy relationships to some emotions, like anger. Often, then, we get surprised by an emotion rising up. Instead of leapfrogging it or stuffing it down because it's uncomfortable, acknowledging the emotion is essential for our growth. It's common to discover an unserving belief system (B.S.) behind the emotion, and it gives us a chance to experience it, first, and then clear it if it no longer serves us.

Sometimes our belief systems label a feeling we're having in a particular way. For example, think about excitement versus anxiety. Often those emotions' physical sensation is the same – some describe it as butterflies in their stomach – but for some reason we typically label it fear. Fear shows up with the unknown and excitement comes with what is known. Often fear is misdiagnosed excitement towards the unknown.

Think about your emotional body: how are you using it in life and work?

The reason that I'm asking you how you're using these energies is to raise your awareness that you CAN use them. Awareness is power. Instead of perceiving life as happening to you, you can use the energies in a constructive way so that life is happening through you.

Knowing that we have these orbs impacting us at any given time gives us a greater understanding of the energies at play in our whole lives. Our sacred calling, for example, is a wild card in relation to The Law of Attraction. If you're doing all the right things, and still not getting what you want, it could be that what you want isn't aligned with your sacred calling. The experience you're here to have may not include that thing you want.

Source directs energy and that gives us infinite possibilities. As humans, we have a limited scope of what's possible. Embracing all of these energies enables possibilities beyond our scope to come in. Awareness of these energies and how to use them will facilitate flow in your life and work.

Notice that I have yet to talk about your career or business. What we've covered so far is essentially an awareness of the playing field you're on. When you put too much burden on your career or business to provide for you, it causes disruption of flow. It's ignoring the other three energies by limiting your scope of being provided for by working. Instead, when you acknowledge all these energies and embrace your work as "a human being walking this planet in service to others" in all areas of your life, flow gets facilitated.

We can no longer live divided lives. As soul-powered people, our successful reach depends upon our ability to integrate our whole selves in all that we do. When I acknowledged that how I interact with the barista at the coffee shop is as important as my work with a client, my energy integrated and became much more powerful. I began to see business growth even though I wasn't doing anything differently. I began to see things smooth out in my personal life and experienced greater ease and peace.

Honoring this integration enables you to see more possibilities. You might be at a cocktail hour with your spouse and meet a potential client. You could organize a group of neighbors to clean up your street and meet someone who has an open position in your field at their company.

I often say that I work 24/7. I don't mean work in the traditional sense. When I say work, I mean fulfilling my sacred calling. When I understand these four orbs are always at play, it releases me to BE and gives me such greater reach. Work is just one place my BEing shows up. When I integrate my BEing in all I do, I place myself in a greater position to receive.

CHAPTER FIVE

Connect to Your Unique iOS

My clients say that I'm the "how to" to the "woo woo." I've been given the gift of putting framework to esoteric concepts. Connecting to your internal Operating System (iOS) is about looking within and stoking the fire of connection with the Source of your understanding.

When most people face a pivot point in life and work, they leap right into doing something… anything! Without this inward look, first, all of that activity might get invested in the wrong place. Others set goals they want to accomplish (again, just doing). Once they meet a goal, they look around for something else they want to do and set another goal. It's a bit like interval training, where you're scrambling fast for a short period of time and then have a period of down time.

Even though this is a common practice, chasing goal after goal, it's exhausting if that's the only concept that you're implementing. A big miss many people make in this goal-setting approach is not choosing goals aligned with them. Action for action's sake is distraction. It is that front-wheel drive compact car I mentioned before that you always feel like you need to push along.

What needs to happen in addition to choosing aligned goals is to put a sustainable "who you be" energy in place that overarches what you do. I call it your iOS or internal Operating System. The elements of your "who you be" iOS include your sacred calling, your personal values, and your Ideal Life Design.

Knowing that these elements will help sustain your energy, motivation, and enthusiasm is a key component of flow. They help you make aligned decisions and stay open to the possibilities. Your iOS is that rear-wheel drive sports car that moves you along effortlessly.

What most people find when they implement these foundational elements is that they're doing less – because they're only choosing aligned inspired action – while getting greater results. Let's look at each foundational element and how you can put them in play for yourself.

Sacred Calling

Instead of Why or Purpose, I like to call this element your sacred calling. There is a lot of misinformation out there about "finding your purpose." It's causing people to constantly run after a carrot on a stick. It's causing people to think purpose is about their work. It's not. You ARE purpose. You are already ON purpose.

Your calling isn't outside of you to be found, it's already inside of you waiting for you to recognize it. Once you realize why you're here on the planet, your whole life makes so much sense. It shows up in all aspects of your life, not just work.

My sacred calling has unfolded into a deeper and deeper meaning over the years. I started out with "Everybody matters and deserves to be heard." Then I realized that it was about having meaningful conversations, because that's an accessible medium everyone can use and be heard within. Then it hit me that I'm really more about keeping human connection alive through the art of conversation. I'm sure it will unfold further as my journey continues and I look forward to gaining an even deeper insight.

The Wise Whys Exercise

One method to discover your sacred calling is to think about a cause you feel strongly about. Let's say that you are committed to rescuing senior dogs.

Ask yourself why this cause is so important.

Let's say that your response to that is that you think it's horrible that people abandon senior dogs at shelters.

Ask yourself why you think it's horrible.

Let's say your response to that is that you believe when you get a pet, you should commit to the pet for life.

Ask yourself why it's important to commit to a pet for life.

Let's say your response to that is you believe that the pet is the person's responsibility and surrendering their pet is going back on their commitment.

Ask yourself, why commitment is so important.

Let's say your response to that is you believe a person's integrity is linked to keeping their commitments.

Ask yourself, why integrity is so important.

As you can see, this process could go on for a while… and it does when I do this work in client sessions. Yet it leads you down a path to better understanding yourself and what drives you to act.

The final question that you ask yourself, once you've moved through asking and answering Why at least five times, is this:

"Why do *I* care that other people act in integrity?"

You see, it's one thing to have your own personal code of conduct and values – it's something else entirely to expect others to act according to your standards. Behind this expectation, is a clue to your sacred calling. Because we are being called to service, our beliefs about other people and what they do or what they need is tied to our sacred calling.

Let's say that your answer is, "I care about people acting in integrity because it facilitates trust, an essential element in strong communities."

Boom. The sacred calling here reflects the person's motivation to build strong communities by facilitating trust. That motivation likely shows up in many other examples in that person's life. This exercise is one of many I use with my clients, and I'm able to see themes that reinforce each other across the different exercises.

It is part of my spiritual belief system that we're here to serve in very specific and meaningful ways. It's a part of your spiritual DNA that's already driving you to act. It's not even a choice. It's something you've been given in terms of talent, skills, abilities, and preferences, yet it has an overarching application.

Because my sacred calling is about keeping human connection alive through the art of conversation, everything that I choose to do is aligned with that calling. I can't help but connect people to resources, people, and opportunities. I teach entrepreneurs messaging and grow their skills at networking, 1-on-1's, negotiation, sales conversations, and public speaking.

I help professionals manage conflict at work and in their personal relationships. I teach them to connect to their Ideal Life Design so they can choose work that supports it. I help them present themselves strongly in interviews so they can contribute their gifts to a company. I teach people-pleasers and empaths how to articulate their needs and set boundaries with others in a constructive way.

Your sacred calling shows up everywhere, not just at work. In my case, I teach adults swing dancing as a hobby. How is that part of my sacred calling? It's all about connection: to their own bodies, to their partners, and to the music. Nothing warms my heart more than seeing a couple dancing, smiling, and working it out on the dance floor.

Start working the Wise Whys Exercise and see how close you can get to recognizing your sacred calling. What I find is that an outside set of eyes is critical because we can't always see ourselves as clearly as others see us. Just like my coach did for me.

Like a physical therapist can push us to stretch our comfort zone, so can someone else asking you the Why questions: they can help you get deep behind your motivations in a way that you can't. My clients are often amazed at where we end up with this exercise. They get a huge "aha" and it helps them with self-acceptance as well as self-awareness.

Personal Values

Our value system is what's behind our choices. Most of us don't take the time to bring our personal values into our conscious awareness. We move through life, doing things and making decisions that reflect our values… without realizing it.

For example, one person might choose the cheapest contractor to paint their house and another person might choose the best contractor to paint their house. Behind each of those decisions is their value system. There's no right or wrong. It's simply what they choose.

One of my values is efficiency and it shows up in all areas of my life. If I'm going to venture out running errands, I'm going to take a progressive loop, logistically, in the order in which I'm going to encounter the stores. When I go grocery shopping, I write my shopping list in the order of how the store is laid out.

What do you value? Make a list of your values so that you can bring them front and center into your conscious awareness.

Make sure that your values list consists of characteristics and not nouns. For example, "family" is not a value system, it's a noun. If you value family because you believe people are better together, then "cooperation" or "collaboration" or "connection" might be the values you list.

Once you take this time to be aware of your values, you can use them actively in your decision-making. When you're faced with a decision, you now can ask yourself, "What decision is aligned with my values?" When determining the potential of a strong connection with a person or company, you can explore whether they share similar values.

Ideal Life Design

One of the reasons that soul-powered people get off track is because they've allowed the need to earn money to drive their decisions. They're so focused on work that they forget to paint a picture of their whole life. Another reason is they've been so focused on work or serving other peoples' needs that they simply haven't taken the time to consider what they want. Sound like you?

Once you broaden the scope from work to life, it acknowledges the possibilities that exist everywhere. Where your sacred calling isn't a choice, it's part of your spiritual DNA, creating your Ideal Life Design allows you to express your free will with choices.

Ask yourself how you want to show up in the world and how you want to live. Some people want to live in a tiny house community while others want to live in a big home.

What do you want your vacations to look like? Where specifically do you want to go? How many vacations a year do you want? Ask yourself how much money you want to make and what causes you want to volunteer for.

When you ask yourself these questions, you're embodying what it would feel like for those things to be present. It's that feeling that resonates outward and communicates a certain vibrational frequency to The Universe. It's that frequency that calls in the opportunities that are aligned.

Another method I like to use when envisioning Ideal Life Design is what I call "A day in the life of me." It's a guided visualization that you create for yourself. You start by seeing in your mind's eye what is present around you when you spend a day in your Ideal Life Design.

Start the visualization with looking around you when you wake up in the morning. What does your bedroom look like? Are you alone or with your partner? What colors are in the room? What do you see out of the window? What do you smell in the air? How do the sheets feel on your body? Do you have pets? If so, what kind? Are they on the bed with you? Do you hear them restlessly waiting for you to open the bedroom door?

Then envision what happens next... then next... then next. Bring in as many senses into the visualization as you can: smells, sounds, textures, tastes, and visuals. By prompting all of the senses, you're embodying the experience as if it is happening.

The last method I'd like to share is what I call "A congratulatory letter to myself." You'll imagine that you're three or five or ten years in the future. Choose the timing that feels right for you. You'll be writing a letter to yourself, congratulating yourself on all that you've accomplished.

As you write the letter, you'll acknowledge all areas of your life: work, relationships, finances, community involvement, and well-being. You might say things like "I'm proud of you for..." and "I'm so amazed that you..." And "It's so heartwarming to see that you..." Just let the writing come out organically. You just might surprise yourself with what comes out onto the page.

Instead of taking a passive approach to life happening to you, these exercises take an active approach to painting a picture of what you want your life to look like. It broadens your scope of decision-making beyond just work and it takes the pressure off of making money and shifts the focus to making a life.

Remember, the reason for these iOS exercises is to recalibrate your BEing to honor who you are... today. You might get your own "aha's" in the process. Once you bring these elements into your consciousness, you begin to communicate more clearly to The Universe. It's your vibrational frequency that draws "like" things to you and these iOS elements are what attunes that vibration.

In addition, they will provide you with the sustainable fuel that will fill your cup, first, before you serve others. They help you choose activities that are aligned with who you are. Using your iOS helps ensure you have all the energy, motivation, and enthusiasm that you need to bring your great service into the world. You now have the agility to pivot when an unexpected aligned opportunity presents itself.

If I set a goal that I'm going to open my business in a specific town, it puts blinders on me because I'm set on those specifics. If I instead ask myself, "Why do I want to open my own business in that town?" I'll come up with a list of values and characteristics instead.

If you really want to work for a few specific companies, it's limiting. When you ask yourself, "Why do these companies appeal to me?" You'll come up with a list of characteristics that are important to you.

You'll likely be able to see how what you want to do is aligned with your calling, values, and Ideal Life Design. That vibration is what gets communicated to The Universe. By looking beyond the what and into the why, your eyes will be open to aligned opportunities and you'll be agile enough to pivot.

One of my clients was a corporate professional who was feeling stuck-in-a-rut. She'd been at the same company for 10 years. She'd owned the same townhome for that time and wondered if she should sell it and move somewhere else. She found herself in relationships with men who didn't seem as invested as she was. There really wasn't anything "wrong" with her life, she simply knew she was in a rut and didn't know how to get out of it.

As we worked together on recalibrating her iOS, she started seeing changes in her outer world. She applied to a new position, which then got put on hold. She met a man unexpectedly, who she began to see. These shifts started happening because we discovered a B.S. that she needed to be perfect in order to be valued.

Two short months after our work together ended, the job came off of hold, and she interviewed for it and got it. She entered a committed relationship with the man she had been seeing. Within a year, she became engaged and they married. He moved into her townhome, which ended up being in a great location for both of them. Her life started flowing again because she honored who she was today, her true value, and shifted the B.S. getting in the way.

Make it a practice to revisit your iOS regularly. I happen to love the change of seasons, so I'll go back to my personal values, sacred calling, and Ideal Life Design four times each year. Because our interests and tastes change over time and because we are constantly evolving, it's likely your iOS will change as well. By recalibrating regularly throughout the year, you can ensure that your vibration adjusts accordingly and continues to communicate clearly to The Universe.

CHAPTER SIX

Align Your DOing with Your BEing

Once you've gotten ready by attuning your iOS, it's now time to align your actions accordingly so you can integrate "who you be" in "what you do." A key thing to know is that there are multiple right answers… and no wrong decisions. No matter what you choose, The Universe will ensure that you stay on your path to fulfill your sacred calling.

When you begin to act differently from this new place of attunement, your monkey mind is likely to kick in. Some people might call this your "ego." I see "ego" as myself as a child. I also see it as an essential function of my limbic brain which is wired for survival. As a result, ego doesn't tend to like change. It's perfectly happy operating in the old way; things were just fine that way, right?

When my ego stimulates my monkey mind, I talk to her as "little Christine." I assure her that everything will be taken care of in this new way of being. I tell her that I've got her back and will be with her the entire way. This practice is a loving way to treat yourself as you begin to step into change.

In addition, the people around you may begin to react to you in ways they hadn't before. Just like the ego, the people around you were quite happy with the way things were. You fit into their reality in a particular way in the past. When you begin to make changes, they might feel upset that their reality is changing.

When you notice people reacting to you differently when you're making changes, you can manage expectations using "call a spade a spade" conversations. It goes something like this: "Mom, I'm practicing some new things to improve my life and my work, so you might notice something different about how I speak and what I do. Can I have your support?"

You might also experience The Universe sending you things that are no longer aligned. My clients often contact me when these things happen because they're feeling confused or frustrated. My take on this occurrence is that The Universe is sensing a change in your vibration and isn't sure it's reading you right because of the change.

When these unaligned opportunities show themselves, you have a chance to confirm your new direction by declining that opportunity. When doing so, you're sending a clear vibration that those things are no longer aligned for you.

These experiences are a natural part of beginning to ease into this new alignment with your iOS. The key is to learn new practices to manage yourself well as you evolve. As you know by now, I'm a "both/and" kinda gal, so there are inner work and outer work practices available to you.

Bust the B.S.

You've already learned how powerful your belief systems (B.S.) are as you were working through your sacred calling, personal values, and Ideal Life Design. B.S. is behind every choice that we make. Since you are always in choice, you get to decide which ones you want to keep and which ones you want to release.

Think back to the example I used about choosing a contractor: one person choosing the cheapest contractor versus someone choosing the high-quality contractor. What's behind these choices are a belief system.

The person choosing the cheapest contractor may do so because they believe they don't have money for a quality contractor – or because they only needed very basic work completed.

The person choosing the high-quality contractor may do so because they believe they need to impress the neighbors – or because they value great design and quality work.

Flow only happens when we can get out of the way of our natural evolution. Constant evolution is in our DNA; we can't help but evolve. Yet these B.S. are of our own construction and can slow down our ability to create our Ideal Life Design or fulfill our sacred calling. Our suffering is caused by resisting our natural evolution.

When you realize a B.S. is at play, you can bring those into your awareness and ask yourself, "Is this serving me?" "Is this mine?" "Is this how I want to operate in life?" "Do I want to keep or release this B.S.?"

Belief Systems are formed starting with childhood and throughout our lives. We most often are not conscious they are even there. Let's use money as an example. If you were raised believing that you have to work hard in order to earn money, that B.S. is going to be operating in the background. Who decided it had to be hard to earn money? Is that really your belief system, or are you adopting it from your parents?

I call those childhood belief systems "implants." Against your awareness, those belief systems were implanted in you at a vulnerable time as a child. You were dependent on your parents at that time and you didn't know you had a choice whether to believe what your parents believed or not.

Traumas often implant belief systems in us as well. Traumas can be big or small and we can respond to different traumas differently. One person's job layoff could be as significant a trauma as another person's emotional abuse. Everything is relative to that individual's experience and the same trauma isn't experienced the same way for everyone.

One of my clients endured a poverty-filled childhood, which triggered his unconscious to kick in a reaction in him to feel responsible for his mother's emotional well-being. We worked to release his B.S. that he's responsible for others' reactions or decisions.

Another client discovered one brief moment in an interaction with her father that caused her to believe she needed to be perfect in order for him to be proud of her. We worked to shift that B.S. which had caused her a lot of anxiety and feelings of low worth.

As you can see, my work with clients can be very therapeutic (though not therapy) and sometimes I'll even reccommend they see a therapist if the trauma is beyond my scope. Sometimes it's our sacred wound that births our sacred calling. Our empowered ability to acknowledge and shift unserving B.S. is what facilitates the integration of our true nature – and facilitates flow.

When I moved to North Carolina, I decided that I wanted to be a paid speaker instead of doing the free speaking circuit. Yet every opportunity I had to be paid for speaking either fell through or was a very cumbersome process. When I realized the heaviness around this change, I knew I needed to look a little deeper as to why it wasn't flowing.

As I self-explored my decision to be a paid speaker, I uncovered a B.S. that I felt undervalued on the free speaking circuit that I had used when living in New Jersey. I also realized that my decision was going against one of my personal values: accessibility. I took the time to shift the B.S. and be open to doing free speaking again.

Within a couple of days with very little effort, I got booked for four free speaking gigs. At the first free gig, I received two new clients afterwards. The second free gig was my first keynote address, which taught me the valuable lesson that I didn't really love speaking on a stage.

The third free gig sparked a joint venture opportunity to teach workshops in their space. The fourth free gig fulfilled my personal value to help people in job search. In the end, they all ended up being highly valuable speaking gigs. Isn't it amazing how opening up to possibilities works?!

Ask Questions

As you can see from my example, self-questioning is a powerful tool. Another way to use questions is in communication with The Universe, which is a call and response system. When you talk about "like attracts like," The Universe doesn't have a choice but to respond to your question; it has no free will. As a result, it's important to ask questions in a way that communicates clearly. By doing so, you can be sure that you're transmitting a resonance that's as aligned with you as possible.

Taking that aligned vibration concept into questions amps up the power even more. Some of the techniques here I learned through the practice of Access Consciousness™ (AC).

Let's use a money example again. If I say "I can't open my senior rescue dog shelter because I don't have the money," then there's a limiting belief system in there. Most people would think that statement is legit, and for most people it is legit because they operate from a limited scope of decision-making. They have a B.S. that you can't act on something until you have the money.

The truth is that anything is possible. What if starting it as a non-profit could get the volunteers and donations needed to start it up? What if I told a friend about my desire and they connected me with a business partner or investor? What if a senior dog rescue non-profit was looking for an executive director?

You can use AC expansiveness questions to activate that call and response system of The Universe. Here are a few formats that I use and like:

"I wonder what it would look like to [receive $500 or more out of the blue this week]? Anything that doesn't allow that, am I ready to uncreate and destroy it now?"

"What energy, space, and consciousness can me and my body be to [receive a steady stream of sustainable income for all eternity]? Anything that doesn't allow that, am I ready to uncreate and destroy it now?"

"What would it take to [go on vacation four times a year for two weeks each]? Anything that doesn't allow that, am I ready to uncreate and destroy it now?"

In the above examples, you can insert whatever you choose in the brackets. These are just examples to show you how to use expansive questioning. You'll also run a "clearing statement" after you answer the last question, which you'll learn about in the next section.

These three different AC expansiveness questions are very powerful as well:

"How does it get any better than this?"

"What else is possible here?"

"What's right about this that I'm not seeing?"

When I ask these expansive questions, I am allowing The Universe to answer them. It ignites a growth mindset in my psyche and prompts me to look beyond my human limited thinking. It prompts The Universe to bring back the most aligned answer, even if it wasn't what I might have pictured.

Some people believe in affirmations, but I'm not completely sold on them. The reason is because many people will state an affirmation without actually believing it. What ends up happening is a vibration of disbelief, which intercepts the intent of the affirmation. I also feel affirmations are limiting because they state a specific outcome and there might be something out there more aligned that isn't yet known.

If you use affirmations, then ensure you actually believe them. If you want to own a senior rescue dog shelter, the traditional affirmation would be to say "I own a senior rescue dog shelter." But if you don't know how in the world that's going to happen and you have doubt, then you're sending out a doubt vibration.

Instead, you can say something like "I'm **going** to own a senior rescue dog shelter." What that sends out is a strong vibration because you're communicating a decision that you've made.

There are many ways to manifest what you want if you would only believe that it's possible and leave the how up to The Universe. That is why questions are so important; you're calling in what's already there but don't see.

Attune Your Vibration

Expansiveness questions are a technique to expand into possibilities and clearing statements bust the B.S. so your vibration is clear. If I realize I'm limiting myself, I'll use this AC clearing question: "Everything that is, am I ready to uncreate and destroy it now?"

Because you're always in choice, you're giving yourself the chance to shift the B.S., even if you aren't sure where it originated. The next part of that practice is a clearing statement to release the B.S., whatever it is. You can visit *www.ClearingStatement.com* to learn the AC method.

I also help my clients create their own clearing statement. The key to it working is your belief that you're releasing the B.S. getting in the way. One of my clients uses the dump truck back-up beeping noise. Another uses "Cancel/Clear/Delete." It's your mind and your made-up B.S. so choose a method that works for you. Have fun with it!

Using a clearing statement or practice shifts any B.S. so that you're keeping your vibration clear. It doesn't require you to remember how you adopted the B.S. I see the clearing practice like blowing up a battleship in a video game. You're always in choice and this practice is you simply choosing to release the B.S.

There are many other modalities available to clear limiting beliefs that may also work for you. Some people use Emotional Freedom Technique (EFT), which is also called tapping. Others use reiki practices or brain retraining courses. Some therapists use Eye Movement Desensitization and Reprocessing (EMDR) or Cognitive Behavioral Therapy (CBT). There are many right answers and it's imperative that you create or choose what feels in alignment with you.

I find that deep belly breathing is a critical tool throughout the use of these practices. Because we are shifting B.S., it will often bring up an emotional response along with it. In some cases, we might even remember the experience we had that created the B.S. If there's an emotional charge with it, it may feel uncomfortable but it's a very good sign.

Where there's emotion, there's learning. The emotion may stimulate your "fight/flight/freeze" response if the memory is stressful. Once you discover the B.S., acknowledge it, then clear it. Using deep belly breathing helps keep you calm throughout the process.

Most of us breathe in our upper lungs or chest. If you watch a baby breathe, you'll see the belly moving up and down, not the chest. For some reason, it's common for adults to begin breathing with our chest instead of our belly. I don't know why this is, but we can relearn belly breathing.

Just sit down and notice your natural breathing. Chances are, you'll notice yourself using your chest. Once you're relaxed, see if you can allow the next inbreath to expand your belly instead of your chest. It may take a few tries, so give yourself some time to get the hang of it.

Once you're filling your belly consistently, begin to count on the inbreath and outbreath. Start first by counting to four for each: four counts for the inbreath and then four counts on the outbreath. This practice grows your awareness of your breathing rhythm.

The next phase of belly breathing is to extend the outbreath longer than the inbreath. This practice stimulates the body's vagus nerve, which turns on our "rest/digest" response. Start by counting to four for your inbreath and then counting to six for the outbreath.

Once that feels rhythmic, then count to four for your inbreath and then count to eight for the outbreath. The extended outbreath is what stimulates the calming effect throughout our central nervous system.

Belly breathing is a tool you can use anywhere at any time. Not only when using the practices, but also during a stressful day at work; or during an argument; or when someone cuts you off in traffic. It's a simple and effective way to bring down your stress response so that you can stay present and responsive instead of reactive.

Since so much of our B.S. is implanted unbeknownst to us, I use a different question when I hear a B.S. in a client: "Is it yours?" This question prompts them to pause and recognize where that belief might have come from. There are two questions to use in those instances: "Everything that is are you ready to uncreate and destroy it now?" or "Shall we return that to sender with love?"

Soul-powered people are especially connected to people in their lives as well as their feelings. They're empathetic and often highly sensitive, which opens them up to potentially carrying others' emotions and beliefs. When we can recognize that is happening, there are some other tools that are helpful as well.

The first tool I like to use is an energy protection practice. As a highly sensitive person – and as one who highly values human connection – I found that I often felt exhausted after interactions with people or groups. I had unknowingly allowed energy hitchhikers.

The two visualizations I invite to use for energy protection are the hazmat suit or hamster ball. I know those sound intriguing, right?! You can use them any time you enter into a group of people, like a party or networking – or when you're dealing with anyone you've felt has been an energy drain in the past.

The hazmat suit visualization is simply you imagining zipping yourself up into a protective suit. Start by stepping into the legs of the suit and pulling it up and putting your arms in. See yourself zipping the suit up all the way to your neck.

The hamster ball visualization is another option when you feel like you want to clear more personal space around you. Just like it sounds, start by getting into a human-sized hamster ball. See yourself walking in the ball with an arms-length diameter of space.

There are times when I forget to use the energy protection practice, and I'll realize that I feel heavy or drained. My friend, Jennifer Urezzio, taught me this energy clearing mantra that I use when that happens:

"I cocreate with the Divine, that all things alien and conditional, leave my mind, body, and spirit at once, and return to their rightful place, with Divine love, will, and grace."

Empowering yourself with these kinds of tools makes you independent and able to regulate yourself as you evolve. Sometimes it's helpful to formally learn them from someone else because another person can often hear the B.S. when we don't. There's never been a time that my clients haven't felt lighter after discovering a B.S. and clearing it. In fact, there's often a lot of laughter when we discover it, because of how ridiculous it sounds!

Stay in Your Service Sweet Spot

As soul-powered people, we sometimes experience a pitfall of wanting to save the world. The reason it's a pitfall is because it's stemming only from our – albeit sincere – desire to help, instead of also considering whether others even want our help.

This savior behavior shows up in both service entrepreneurs and corporate professionals. The reason it's so prevalent is because most of us operate from a belief system (B.S.) that if we DO more, we'll be VALUED more. (this is the time to run your personal clearing statement!)

There's nothing further from the truth. Your value comes simply from being here now. There's nothing that needs to be done in order to prove or earn your value. You are already of high value because your value comes from your connection to Source not your delivery of Service.

As a result, it's important to recognize where your personal sweet spot of service is. I'm going to use a service entrepreneur's example, so if you're a corporate professional then just translate this approach to your workplace or home life.

To find your sweet spot, you need to look at the intersection of several components: Who are you? Who are they? What do you do? What do you say?

When you bring your unique self into the world, there's going to be a unique set of people who are going to resonate with your approach and personality. You aren't the answer for everybody. Once you create a list of characteristics that are in common with you and them, you then decide which part of your service that group of people wants.

You likely could do a lot of things, but the key here is to choose what they want in addition to what you're best at doing and what you enjoy. Only then can you decide how to convey your service as a solution. Only then will you be able to focus, begin to gain traction, and see results.

The reason that this approach works is because you're taking the time to align your actions with you. It's a win-win because you're expressing your best talents and they're most appreciative because they welcome that solution. It isn't about doing whatever they want, it's about serving yourself and them in a way that honors everyone.

For soul-powered entrepreneurs, there will always be outliers or clients just outside of your sweet spot. Yet now you can proceed with greater awareness of where the disconnect could possibly be if they become a client. It's important to stick with the sweet spot, however, and allow the outliers to be drawn to you – instead of going after the outliers. When you keep your vibration clear with your sweet spot as the center point, you know that anything being drawn to you is in alignment.

This is the same approach I use with professionals as they deal with job search, a difficult boss, or challenging work environment. Finding that intersection or sweet spot fuels their confidence which helps them communicate strongly in interviews or during difficult conversations. They often think they want to change jobs. Yet sometimes, once they move through this process, they realize that by shifting their B.S. and learning new communication methods, they are much happier with themselves and at work.

Occasionally, this process helps them recognize they are in the wrong career or industry because it's revealed how much they're stretching outside of their sweet spot at work. I use a test called Multiple Natures (*www.MultipleNatures.com*) to support them further. Multiple Natures (MN) tests their strengths and preferences and generates a list of careers that are most aligned with them. It's a great addition to this sweet spot work for professionals who are facing a career pivot point.

One last example of aligned DOing for soul-powered entrepreneurs is designing the right messaging and business development ecosystems. So often I see entrepreneurs using canned elevator pitches or business models that don't express their uniqueness.

By developing messaging that is sincere and compelling, it draws aligned leads, clients, and opportunities to them. That is enhanced when we also put the right activities for them in their business development ecosystem.

Networking is one of the most common business development activities and one of the most misused. Not everyone shows up strongly in that kind of environment and some that do, aren't using it efficiently or effectively. A good business development ecosystem will facilitate that flow of leads, clients, and opportunities – so the activities need to be aligned with the entrepreneur.

One of my clients is a very strong introvert and doesn't like networking. So we built an ecosystem that starts with her teaching classes and then inviting the students into 1-on-1 conversations.

One client loves to speak, so we built an ecosystem to help her convert the room. Another client is a master networker, so we built an ecosystem that starts with her hosting private VIP networking events to find joint venture and strategic alliance opportunities.

These practices help you keep your vibration clear by shifting the B.S. and asking questions to ignite the power of possibilities from The Universe. It's embracing who you are and aligning what you do with YOU, instead of the other way around, which causes burnout. It allows you to do fewer yet more aligned actions. These practices strengthen your agility in all aspects of your life, enabling you to pivot when opportunities come your way that you didn't foresee.

CHAPTER SEVEN

Navigate the Possibilities

We've moved through getting ready by recalibrating your iOS. You've learned how to get set with aligned DOing. Flow is learning how to navigate life and work as you're using these new practices.

Imagine yourself floating down a river on an inner tube. You're going to encounter rapids, slow segments, going in circles in an eddy, as well as smooth and easy times. It's inevitable that there will be a mix of experiences as you float down the river: the good, the bad, and otherwise. It's also exactly how life happens. The key is how you navigate those perceived good, bad, slow, tumultuous, smooth, and stagnant waters of life.

I don't love acronyms, so I know when Spirit hands them to me that they're especially meaningful and powerful. I grew up in an Army family, so I knew what MREs and BDUs were. I spent 20 years in corporate and each company had their sets of acronyms, too. I got really good at them. Once I left corporate and saw the overuse of acronyms in the coaching/consulting industry, I didn't like it at all. Yet, like E.F. Hutton, when The Universe talks, I must listen.

FLOW stands for:
Flexibility
Levity
Openness
Wonderment

Flexibility

I find that soul-powered people have a multitude of interests. Many judge themselves for not sticking to one thing or not finishing things. Once you've implemented the practices in the preceding sections, it gives you the agility you need to be flexible. Using your intuition to sense what feels aligned for you will guide your choices. You might have 50 things you're working on, but when you use your new practices before making a choice, it amps up your intuition and gives you the flexibility that you need and you can trust yourself.

A client messaged me the evening after her session and said, "You know, Christine, every time we get off a call something crazy aligned happens." She said, "I was supposed to pay this invoice for a service person to come and start remodeling the house that my new husband and I are moving into, but something told me to wait."

So, she trusted what she was being guided to do and she waited. Later that evening, the deal on the place they were moving to fell through. If she had pushed her intuition aside and paid the contractor invoice, she would have entered into a formal agreement with the contractor. Trusting your intuition, even when you don't know why it's telling you something, is a wonderful gift to give yourself.

Levity

What I know for sure is that Spirit doesn't work in heavy energy. When we are faced with decisions and can't seem to make one, we can put pressure on ourselves and that can also feel heavy. Using these practices allows you to make a clear connection to Source. When you embody them into your life and your work, you'll be better equipped to sense the energetic lightness that will direct your choice.

Levity also means humor, fun, and joy. I've learned that Joy is an essential element in manifestation. When you're able to keep things light and not take yourself or your journey too seriously, it opens up the connection pathway to Source. When an amazing opportunity comes in, I like to say, "Thank you, Universe, more please!" The levity of that helps reinforce for The Universe what you're getting is what you want.

And, oh, by the way, if you're using the practices and still aren't getting a clear answer, then set it aside until you do. If it's not a "hell yeah!" then it's a "no" for now.

If money is tight and you're worrying about being able to pay your bills, you're bringing heavy energy into the equation. Worry is a vibration that you don't want to be transmitting because it's what you'll get back. Instead, see if you can bring in a few of those AC expansiveness questions. Sometimes I'll even adopt a childlike persona to ask questions when I realize I'm in heavy energy. Once I use a few questions and clear the B.S., it recalibrates my vibration into lightness.

Openness

Knowing that The Universe has infinite possibilities at its disposal enables you to expand your mind beyond what you can see or think. When you allow yourself to be open and take those limiting blinders off, you'll be amazed at what comes into your reality. Now remember, I'm not telling you to throw all the practical goals and planning in the trash. Using these tools at your disposal allows you to be more open so that you can see the possibilities as they arrive.

One of my clients had put a financial plan in place to pay off some credit card debt. He had also moved through creating his Ideal Life Design. Part of that vision was living in an apartment in a particular town. During one of his sessions, he told me how he had serendipitously come upon a fabulous apartment for rent in that very town, but that he decided against it because the timing wasn't right with his current lease.

When I pressed him about the timing, he also added that taking the apartment would interrupt paying back the credit card debt. I said, "So, your dream apartment falls into your lap and you're going to pass because of your financial plan?" Mind you, that was not said in a judgmental tone, just to help him hear what I was observing. I also said, "The right answer just may be to pass on the apartment, but I want you to make the decision from a harmonized place of intuitive and logical – not just logical."

Guess what? He left the session, worked these practices, and decided to have two leases for a short period of time and reduce the credit card pay-back plan so he could take advantage of his dream apartment.

Wonderment

When we fully surrender to the four orbs of living (remember those? Spiritual, Metaphysical, Physical, and Emotional), it frees us to step back and watch in amazement how our lives unfold. Asking questions with sincere childlike curiosity about what the answer might end up being. "I wonder what it would look like..."

The wonderment comes from being unattached to an expected outcome. If we can really stay in that childlike joy and wonderment, The Universe is given permission to bring back a truly wonderous answer.

Take, for example, the client who found his dream apartment. Once he and his husband moved into the new apartment, his business started to shift and grow without doing much differently.

You see, when we choose ourselves and step into expansiveness in our personal lives, it flows into all areas of our lives because we're now living an integrated life with these practices. It's wonderous! Once he made the decision to invest in himself and expand his personal life, his business life also expanded. How does it get any better than that?!

Here's a client example that demonstrates how to navigate the possibilities in a situation. As you read it, mark the sentences that represent the different practices and concepts that you've learned so far:

One of my clients was ready to bring on another employee. I was helping her with the candidate screening. We interviewed a candidate and decided to make him an offer, which he accepted. His start date was a few weeks out so that he could give notice at his former company and help the transition.

Ten days later, he sent her an email explaining why he couldn't take the position after all. When she contacted me to let me know, she was upset about what happened. As I coached her through the emotion, she was able to recognize that she was actually afraid she wouldn't find a good candidate for the position. We allowed the fear, then ran the clearing statement to shift the B.S. that was limiting her. She did some deep belly breathing and she felt lighter.

I gave her the homework to create two organizational charts: one for the current year and one for the next year. Because she was forecasting very large revenue growth, I told her to calculate how many employees she would need for each year, and the types of positions she would need, in order to meet those revenue goals. I then said, "How does it get any better than this?!"

Within a week, she called me all excited, saying "I may have just found an even better candidate!" Someone she'd known in her industry for quite a while contacted her out of the blue a few weeks prior because he was looking to change jobs. At that time, though, she was waiting for the prior candidate to be able to start. Now, she could consider him!

She was concerned, however, because he was much more experienced than she needed right now. I asked her, "Is he one of the positions that you have on your org chart for next year?" She said, "Yes." I started laughing and she asked me what I was laughing about.

I said, "Do you see how clearly you communicated to The Universe your revenue goals and the team members you needed to reach them? The Universe must have big plans for you, because it sent you the right person... just a year early!"

We both laughed at the synchronicity and then we got to work crunching numbers to see how she could bring him on board now. We interviewed him, made him an offer, and he accepted.

In this example, her Ideal Business Design is what drew in the right candidate. Acknowledging the emotion and shifting the underlying B.S. cleared her vibrational frequency. Her unattachment to the outcome with the prior candidate withdrawing is what allowed her to be agile enough to bring on a more experienced candidate a year earlier than planned.

Embracing these elements of Flow helps you navigate the practical world with a spiritual approach. Instead of bending to conform with our job, partner, or business, we're litmus testing those outer opportunities to see if they're in alignment with our inner BEing. Remaining unattached to a pictured outcome and surrendering to the possibilities that show themselves allows us to get out of the way of our natural evolution.

CHAPTER EIGHT

Embody Your True Value

Have you gotten beaten down by life or work and lost sight of your brilliance? Do you equate your worth to the level of your bank account? Are you facing health challenges and wondering why this is happening to you? You might be caught up in those beliefs because you don't yet know your true value.

Many people around us are following the illusions they're being taught. They might be limiting what they do in their life because they don't have the money or because they're afraid to change careers. They're often believing the fear and scarcity that our media feeds them. How about you?

You've heard my philosophy and how to unattach from others' beliefs so you can flow. What follows is one final piece that can't be overlooked: your relationship with money.

I'm not saying that your true value is reflected by your relationship with money. I am saying that I often uncover a B.S. in soul-powered people that if they do more they'll be valued more. This un-serving belief system is part of what interrupts their flow of money.

You are already of full value just by being here. You're already a part of Source. You are already whole and complete. Your connection to Source and bringing your sacred calling into the world is your true value. Once you really know that to be true, your relationship with money can transform.

One way to more fully embody your true value is to shift your relationship and limiting beliefs about money so that it's aligned with your true value. Money can be a delicate topic for many people. We live in a world that requires money from us. For soul-powered people, it is often the last big integration lesson that will unleash the flow of money.

Are you ready to shift your money story by recognizing your true value? If so, then it's time to better understand how your embodiment of your true value shows up in money form.

When I ask people where money comes from, they'll immediately respond "from working." But when I press further and ask them when they've ever received money without working for it, they'll pause for a moment and then reply with one or more of these examples: I got money for my birthday; I received an inheritance; I won money in the lottery; I got money as a gift; I found money on the sidewalk. Immediately, I'm able to bust their B.S. that money only comes from working.

John Randolph Price says we aren't compensated on our activity of work, we're compensated on our activity of consciousness. Consciousness is awareness that Source is your supply, not your work. Compensation doesn't mean money, it means to compensate for. Something must move in when something moves out; it is simply how The Universe operates. Yet, it's not exclusively reciprocal. When you give, you could be compensated from anywhere.

One huge pitfall for soul-powered people is that they often don't know how to receive. They are so wired for giving and serving that they can simply be unfamiliar with receiving. How often do you let people buy you coffee or a meal? How comfortable are you with receiving? By not receiving, you are interrupting the law of compensation and unknowingly communicating to The Universe that you don't want more.

"Once you make a decision, The Universe conspires to support you."
—RALPH WALDO EMERSON

What if making the decision to spend money is what brings in more money? If you're hoarding money, or not spending it because you're fearing not having enough, you're guaranteeing you won't get more. If you instead use or assign your money, you're guaranteeing you'll get more.

Once you fully embody this concept of living an integrated life, you'll begin to experience compensation of your true value in some amazing ways. Just like my client and his dream apartment: once he made a decision to invest in himself personally, he received compensation with new business growth.

Why does it work this way? Because you are finally acknowledging your worth by serving your needs and desires, which transmits a frequency of value, which draws value to you. The root of the word "wealth" is "well-being" or "welfare." Making your well-being a priority brings you wealth.

Here are a few foundational money practices that demonstrate these beliefs:

- **Set up different banking accounts for different purposes**. Then, on a regular basis, move money into those different accounts that are earmarked for a purpose: it might be saving up for a new car or putting money aside for a vacation or creating a business fund to prepare for growth. The Universe reads that movement of money as being used and more flows in to compensate for that usage.

- **Set up an account that honors your ever-increasing value.** Move a consistent amount of money into an account that you won't touch. Choose either a percentage of earnings, I use 10%, or a set dollar amount. The amount doesn't matter; the practice of moving it into the account does. It's not a savings account or a back-up account, it's not to be used. This practice teaches us what "appreciation" really means: both increasing in value and gratitude.

- **Keep a large denomination bill in your wallet.** Use a $100 bill if you can or a $50 if that's more aligned for you. This bill isn't to be tucked away in a dark crevice somewhere for a rainy day. It's to be kept with your other money and not spent. Every time you open your wallet, you get that pleasant surprise of seeing a large denomination bill. It gives you the experience of always having money.

- **Create a "dashboard" spreadsheet of your money (or use an online budgeting tool).** List all of your bank accounts and investments and the amount of money in them. List each of your credit cards, including the total credit limit, the balance owed, and the remaining credit limit available. Include car loans or home mortgages. List the money coming in (income) and the money flowing out (expenses). Include a section to record non-monetary receipts, like that lunch someone bought you. This dashboard shows you how your money flows.

- **Valuate your Ideal Life Design.** Create a "current" section and create a "future" section in your dashboard. In the future section, list specifics that are part of your Ideal Life Design. For example, list the cost of your future vacation home or list the new income you're expecting. Calculate the difference between current and future and highlight that number. This approach communicates the energetic frequency of what it will take to manifest your Ideal Life Design from where you are.

By shifting your money B.S. in these ways, you're amping up the power of the practices outlined in this book. You're taking your power back from your job/boss or your business and taking the burden off, expecting them to provide for you. You're owning that only you can shift your money story. The same Bust the B.S. practices work in your money story as well... use them!

CHAPTER NINE

CHAPTER NINE

Integrate Your New Practices

You might be saying, "Yeah, right, Christine. This all sounds well and good, but the rest of the world doesn't operate this way." Or "This sure is an idealistic way to be, it sounds too good to be true." What I would tell you is:

"Whether you think you can, or think you can't, you're right."

–Henry Ford

These are called practices for a reason… you have to practice them! The best way to start is one step at a time in the order you've learned them in this book. Try them and see if they work. Every section gives you practices you can start right away. At this end of this chapter, I've created a summary you can use to strengthen your practice.

When you act from a place of inspired action that's aligned with you, you are communicating your decision and intentions to The Universe. Being unattached to a specific outcome enables you to surrender to whatever is happening. In a way, it's like having an out-of-body experience: you're now able to look at what's showing up in your life in a very objective way.

By honoring your intuition when making decisions, you release expectations of what will come of the decision. Now you know that when you feel triggered emotionally, you're actually being shown a place to practice self-love so that trigger doesn't get in your way anymore. There's a saying, "The only way out, is through."

When you show up intentionally in all areas of your life with this new integrated approach, you're being a contribution to yourself and others. You get to trust yourself and your decision because you know it came from a strong connection to Source.

Being this independent gives you the agility to pivot when possibilities appear. I use these practices every single day. I run clearing statements multiple times a day when I recognize a B.S. that I want to release. I tell my clients that I'm "workin' it" every day, just like they are… I might just be one big toe ahead of ya.

It's incredibly courageous to learn and use these practices in the world today. It certainly goes against the norm. As soul-powered people, we highly value relationships with others. It might feel hard to tell someone you made a decision from your gut and that you don't know why you needed to.

Yet, the more you practice these practices, the more confident you'll become in those conversations. I often say "I don't know why, I just felt led to do it." This level of trusting yourself and your connection to Source is liberating. One of my clients said he didn't realize how exhilarating this flow thing could be – that being unattached to everything is freeing!

Security and safety when attached to another entity is an illusion. In reality, you aren't dependent on anyone else: a job, a business, a company, a spouse. The only stability you have is what you create for yourself in your connection with Source – and navigating them using the practices in this book.

Here's a summary to reference so you can strengthen your new practices:

The Four Orbs of Soul-Powered Living

Spiritual
Metaphysical
Physical
Emotional

Connect to Your Unique iOS

Sacred Calling
Personal Values
Ideal Life Design

Align Your DOing with Your BEing

Bust the B.S.
Ask Questions
Attune Your Vibration
Stay in Your Service Sweet Spot

Navigate the Possibilities

Flexibility
Levity
Openness
Wonderment

Embody Your True Value

BEing Not DOing
Where Money Comes From
Receiving
Money Practices

When you're feeling triggered, use this method as part of your practice:

- Notice that something has triggered you emotionally
- Identify the emotion that's arising
- Acknowledge the emotion and be with it a moment
- Use deep belly breathing to bring in calm
- Determine, if you can, the belief system behind it
- Run a clearing practice to shift it
- Remind yourself of your Unique iOS
- Ask an expansiveness question
- Be ready to pivot when something aligned presents itself

Get Ready. Get Set. Flow... is about the integration of spiritual and practical. It's blending your beliefs with inspired actions that you take in life and in work. It feeds everything in your life so that you have all the energy, motivation, and enthusiasm that you want.

It attunes your intuition so you're making choices that are in alignment with your iOS: your sacred calling, personal values, and Ideal Life Design. By honoring yourself as an essential component of your soul-powered service, you're able to give from a place of overflow instead of a place of depletion. That's a gift that serves you and everyone around you... forever.

Thank you, Universe, more please!

CHAPTER TEN

The Connection Experiment: My Personal Case Study

In October of 2018 I was stricken by a mysterious illness. At first, it looked like I had developed severe environmental allergies. It morphed into me having anaphylactic-like reactions to foods and sometimes they happened out of the blue. I began to feel light-headed and dizzy, sometimes coming close to passing out. My GI tract was out of whack (I'll spare you those details, ha!). My joints became unstable, especially my knees, and I found it challenging to walk without pain. My muscles were constantly seizing up and feeling chronically weak and sore.

Feeling so unwell and being so limited, physically, I was unable to speak as my typical primary marketing channel. I'd been talking about writing this book for a long time, but I didn't feel I had the luxury of focusing on writing. I'm a single entrepreneur, solely dependent on myself to provide for me. Self-publishing a book is a huge under-taking of time, energy, and money. (hear any B.S. in any of that?!)

Yes, I needed to step back into my expansive thinking, so I posed this question to The Universe: "I wonder what it would look like to self-publish my book by the end of this year and have a steady stream of sustainable income? And anything that doesn't allow that, am I ready to uncreate and destroy it now?"

The answer I received was to crowdfund the cost of self-publishing. When I heard this answer, I knew it was Spirit because I would have never asked people to help me pay for my book. I spent $5,000 on my last book publishing – that's a lot of money! Plus, I didn't want people thinking that I was desperate. I had the resources to fund self-publishing myself, just like I did last time.

I ignored the answer. Yet, as I was working my practices, I was led to use a lead-generation tool on LinkedIn. Within the first couple of weeks, I landed several new clients. I would never have thought to use that LinkedIn tool, yet Spirit prompted me to consider it. It became my primary stream of income over the Summer of 2019 as I continued dealing with my health issues.

If my question for a sustainable stream of income was answered, then why was I ignoring the answer to crowdfund the self-publishing of my book? In short, it was because I was worried about what other people thought. I didn't want to be one of those desperate fundraisers because I wasn't desperate.

So, I asked another question: What else is possible here? In truth, I thought I'd get a different answer! Guess what? I got the same answer with a further message: Spirit told me that this effort was not about the money… it was about connection! By offering the book fundraiser, I was giving other people a way to connect with me. Whoah!

Just like Spirit gave me the FLOW acronym, I knew this message was true because I would never have chosen it for myself. As I've taught in this book, I knew I was in choice and that I didn't have to choose crowdfunding my book. Yet, I've always been taken care of, as evidenced by the recent LinkedIn leads, so why wouldn't I trust this option as well?

I spent the summer resisting this guidance and by early August, I knew I needed to surrender to the effort. I wrote at least three different versions of the Go Fund Me campaign page. Each time, I was trying not to sound desperate. On the fourth version, I knew I was much closer and it started feeling light. I sent it off to a dear friend to proofread for me and I closed my computer to step away from the task for a bit. My girlfriend gave me the thumbs up on that version, but when I came back to the page, the fourth version wasn't there! I had forgotten to hit SAVE.

After cursing up a blue storm and allowing my emotion to be experienced, I settled into my practices. I asked myself "What's right about this that I'm not seeing?" and "What else is possible here?" What came forth after those questions was a fifth version that felt extremely light and right on the mark for the essence I wanted to convey! How does it get any better than that?!

I decided to launch the fundraiser near my birthday, prior to Labor Day Weekend. I started by sending out a newsletter to my community. For the first hour after that email was sent, I watched as I reached a 50 percent open rate... but no one clicked through to the fundraiser. Ugh! I started to feel vulnerable and anxious. I started to second guess doing the fundraiser.

I stepped away from the computer and began to use my practices to clear the B.S. and uncertainty. I talked to little Christine to let her know all was going to be well. I reminded myself to release any attachment to the outcome. After about 20 minutes, I began to feel the heaviness lift, so I went back to the computer, refreshed the page, and what did I see?

$2,500 in the fundraiser! What?! I literally rubbed my eyes because I couldn't believe I was seeing what I was seeing! I scrolled down and saw that a dear friend made one donation for $2,500, wow. Just wow. I started crying from disbelief and then from awe about what just happened. I picked up the phone and immediately called her to thank her profusely for her donation. She told me that I was the best investment she could think of making.

Within only 10 days, the book was 70 percent funded. It was fascinating to see who felt led to connect and contribute to me. A past subcontractor. Another dear friend. My brothers. A colleague. My father. An acquaintance on LinkedIn. Several clients. A neighbor.

For a couple of weeks, I received no donations. I worked my practices to release the outcome. Along the way, I kept checking in with my intuition to see if there was any additional promotion I was supposed to be doing. I kept getting a "no." With very little effort, my book was 100 percent funded for $5,000 in five short weeks.

This example shows most of the components that I've taught you in this book. Even though I'm an entrepreneur, the same practices apply if you're a corporate professional or a Domestic CEO. I work these practices every single day with a variety of circumstances: from listening to a prompt to take something with me when I leave the house – to making a decision about a doctor, supplement, modality, or test for health care.

I know that I must be experiencing this chronic illness for a reason; my spiritual beliefs are that we're meant to have all the experiences, good, bad, and otherwise. There certainly were times over this past year when I was shaking my fist at Source and so despondent about my condition that I couldn't function. There have definitely been money concerns because I'm choosing many natural approaches that aren't covered by insurance. That simply makes me human. As I encounter each B.S., I work my practices.

I'm using a truly integrated approach to my health, both traditional and complimentary medicine. (See how my both/and beliefs show up here, too?) I may have a connective tissue dysfunction, so it makes it difficult to get a specific diagnosis. While I'm seeking one because I feel it's medically responsible, I know that all I need is to listen to my intuition to guide me.

I've been able to stabilize my physical and mental health and I'm improving a little more each and every day. I can honestly say this health crisis is the single most challenging thing I've faced in my life so far. Doctors don't believe me or brush off my symptoms or get defensive when I come in with my research.

What *Get Ready. Get Set. Flow...* has given me is the knowing that I don't need their validation. I just KNOW there's something misfiring in my body – and I'm going to figure it out. I use these practices throughout it all and they help ground me into the knowing that all is as it should be.

If you're so inspired, I invite you to go back through my story – using the summary in Chapter 9 – and see if you can spot the practices I've shared in this book. Most of all, I hope you feel inspired to give the gift of *Get Ready. Get Set. Flow...* to yourself.

About the Author

Christine Clifton is a Flow Facilitator. She believes in the power of connection: to Source, Self, and Service. When this connection is fostered, anything is possible!

A 20-year veteran of chronic illness, Christine had to learn practical coping skills as well as spiritual expansion practices in order to surThrive. She became an efficiency expert and designed her own methods because the traditional models she had been taught in career and entrepreneurship simply exhausted her.

As a result, she's dedicated to teaching soul-powered people how to keep their inner fire burning so they don't burn out. The world is CHEATED without their voice and work in it!

They often over-give in order to feel of value... and they skip over serving themselves. This bypass causes stagnancy, aimlessness, and burnout because they've lost their awareness of their own evolution – and who they are... today. By facilitating their connection to their calling, Christine teaches them to better align their practical DOing with their natural BEing to find flow in their work, health, and life again.

Get her free training, "Ignite Your Inner Leader" at www.ChristineClifton.com.

In addition to *Get Ready. Get Set. Flow...*, she's the author of *You don't have to shout to Stand Out* and *Your Spirit at Work*. She became a natural student of human behavior and motivators during her 20-year management career and current 13 years of entrepreneurship. Christine holds an MBA in Marketing and a BA in Business Administration and is also a graduate of Coach U. She's a Certified

Multiple Natures Practitioner, a Certified Reiki master, and a Certified Access Bars Practitioner. Christine is highly connected to energy flow, which helps her work with her clients to navigate using their intuition.

As an inspirational speaker, her fresh, interactive approach engages audiences with her stories, lessons, and wit. She can be found tooling around Saxaphaw, NC, in JOY, her spice orange, MINI Cooper convertible; eating at the area farm-to-table restaurants; and listening to local musicians play.

Christine is available for seminars, retreats, and speaking engagements.

Contact her at
Christine@ChristineClifton.com
or 201-738-7463.

CPSIA information can be obtained
at www.ICGtesting.com
Printed in the USA
FSHW010925170420
69294FS